My First Puppy

ROSMARIE HAUSHERR

FOUR WINDS PRESS/NEW YORK

*A big thank-you to Tom, Robbie, and Ben Lewis—
and an even bigger one to Jenny Lewis and Molly—for
their enthusiastic participation in the demanding
photo sessions necessary for this project.*

*Professional assistance was generously given by
veterinarians Dr. John A. Stetson and Dr. Gail
Zausner; Elizabeth P. Gordon, City Dog Obedience
School; Joe Gordon, Red Doors Kennels; and the staff
of the Bide-a-Wee Home Association in New York City
and Wantagh, New York.*

*I am grateful to Raymond Marunas, who helped
with the writing, and to The Corlears School, Albert
Simmons, Jimmy Falcone, Chip Conrad, William J.
Lederer, Dilys Evans, the Athenaeum librarians, and
many friends for their help.*

*My warm thanks to Catherine Stock for a truly
professional book design.*

Four Winds Press
Macmillan Publishing Company
866 Third Avenue, New York, NY 10022
Collier Macmillan Canada, Inc.
First Edition   10 9 8 7 6 5 4 3 2 1
Printed in the United States of America
The text of this book is set in 14-point Century
Schoolbook. The illustrations are black-and-white
photographs reproduced in halftone.
Library of Congress Cataloging-in-Publication Data
Hausherr, Rosmarie.   My first puppy.
   Summary: Photographs and text follow a girl as she
selects her first puppy and learns about its feeding,
grooming, training, and medical care. A section for
parents discusses where and how to acquire a dog,
spaying and neutering, various aspects of home care,
and suggested rules for children.
   1. Puppies — Juvenile literature. [1. Dogs] I. Title.
SF426.5.H38   1986   636.7′07   86-14979
ISBN 0-02-743410-9

My name is Jenny. My stuffed animals are my favorite toys.

I love animals. There are many in our backyard: snails with pretty shells, ladybugs, butterflies, sometimes even small toads. I wish I could play with them, but they are not pets.

I live with my mom, dad, and younger brother, Ben, on Governor's Island in New York Harbor. We take a ferry to school in Manhattan. From its deck we see cargo ships, tugboats, and barges. Coming home, I feed crumbs from my lunch box to the sea gulls.

Our neighbor Al has a poodle named Trilby. When we

meet she wags her short tail. She knows me because I
help take care of her when Al is away.

When Al and I take Trilby for walks, people tell me I
have a nice dog.

But Al and Trilby are moving to another city. That
makes me sad. I wish I had my own dog.

My birthday is next month. I'll be eight years old. I'm sure that's old enough to have a pet.

I show Dad a picture I've drawn of Trilby. "Daddy, for my birthday, can I have a puppy?"

Dad lifts me to his lap. I can tell he's really thinking. "Well, Jenny, that's a big wish. I'm not sure we are ready to have a dog. Remember, it would live with us for many, many years and need feeding, walking, grooming, and training, which is a lot of work and costs a lot of money. Let me talk with Mom. We need to think about it."

At least he hasn't said no. I bounce up and down, saying, "I'll feed the puppy. I promise."

A few days later, Dad says, "Jenny, Mom and I have decided you may have a puppy for your birthday."

Oh, I'm so happy! I hug my dad and run to find my mom.

She comes into the living room with Ben, carrying books. "I borrowed these from the library," Mom says. "Let's find out what kind of dog would be good for a family like ours."

There are photographs of many *breeds,* or kinds, of dogs. Dad explains that dogs have so many different shapes and sizes because long ago they were bred for different jobs. Big dogs would guard herds or houses, fast runners made good hunters, and small dogs could stalk animals underground. Now most dogs are pets. I like learning about the breeds, but I already know what kind of dog I want. I want a poodle just like Trilby.

That's all right with my mom and dad, especially after we read that poodles are smart, friendly, and good with children.

"Where will we get my puppy, Mom?" I ask. "From a pet store?"

Mom shakes her head. "We'd rather adopt one from an *animal shelter.*"

I'm not sure what a shelter is, and neither is Ben. Mom explains that it's a place where people bring pets they can no longer keep, and some shelters also take in *strays,* animals without owners that live in the streets. All animals are checked by veterinarians, and the healthy ones can be adopted.

We are adopting our puppy from the Bide-a-Wee Home in Wantagh, New York. Dad will go there first and tell them what kind of dog we want.

"We hope they'll have a puppy in time for your birthday," Mom says. "Meanwhile, we have to read more about puppy care and then get ready."

We make a list of things a puppy needs: puppy food, special dishes, a collar and leash, a brush and comb, clippers to trim the puppy's nails, old towels, a box for a bed, and lots of newspapers.

Mom lets me choose the dishes myself, telling me to make sure they are large and sturdy so they won't tip over. I pick two dishes: brown for food and yellow—my favorite color—for water.

Two days before my birthday, a call comes from Bide-a-Wee. I was afraid they had forgotten about my puppy!

"Yes, we are looking for a puppy," Mom says. "Yes.... We'll be there in the morning. Thank you for letting us know."

"Oh, Mom," I beg, "can't we go now?"

"Jenny, be patient. We'll go tomorrow when Dad can come, too."

That night, I am so excited I can hardly sleep.

In the morning Ben and I get ready. Ben spreads newspapers on the kitchen floor, and I put towels into the puppy bed Dad made from a cardboard box. Finally we are ready to go. We are taking our car on the ferry.

"Why do people give their pets away?" I ask.

"I suppose there are many reasons," Mom says. "It takes a lot of patience to train a dog. Some people don't realize that. Sometimes people move and can't take their pets with them. Or their pet has a large litter and they can't find homes for them all. People even develop allergies to their pets, or they just run out of money for food."

"We'll keep our doggy, won't we Jenny?" Ben says. I smile at him. Ben doesn't like animals as much as I do, but he's excited about the puppy, too.

We hear dogs barking as we enter the shelter. The young man at the desk shows us to a large, well-lit room. Puppies of all sizes are in cages along the walls. Some bark, a few are sleeping, but most watch us quietly.

"They are so cute, I wish we could take them all," I say to Dad, and he laughs.

We walk from cage to cage. Mom points out two German shepherd puppies. Dad is looking at a black puppy with brown spots. Ben jumps and grabs Dad's leg when a dog near him gives a sudden loud bark.

A woman comes into the room and greets us. Her name is Debbie. She wants to know if I'm the birthday girl.

"Have you seen the puppy over here?" she asks. "It's the one I called you about." She takes a little white dog from its cage.

"It's a little lamb," Ben says.

Debbie laughs. "It's a healthy female poodle, about eleven weeks old." She puts the puppy gently into my arms. How soft and warm it feels.

"This is the puppy I want," I tell Mom and Dad. "Please!"

"Yes, we'll take her home right now," Ben adds.

My parents smile. "I guess that's our new dog," Dad says, and Mom agrees.

We go into another room where Dad has to sign some forms called *adoption papers*. Then we can take my new puppy home.

"Thank you," I say to Mom and Dad. "Thank you for my puppy."

"What will you call her?" Ben asks.

"Molly," I tell him. "Her name is Molly."

In the car the little dog sits quietly in my lap on towels with a plastic underneath, just in case....

"Speak softly to Molly," Mom says. "Pet her gently behind her ears or on her chest. It will help her not to be afraid. It's new and scary for her to ride in a car with people she doesn't know."

Ben starts singing "Molly, Molly, Molly," and the puppy falls asleep. Being adopted has tired her out.

When we get home I look around for my friends. Too bad none of them are out to see my new puppy.

Before we go inside, Dad shows me how to carry Molly. "Slip one arm under her rear end and back legs," he says, "and support her chest with the other one. Remember, be gentle. If she doesn't want to be carried, leave her. Never grab a leg or pull her tail. That hurts."

I carry Molly very carefully into the kitchen and put her down on the newspapers. She sure is a heavy puppy. Her head and feet are large. My parents say she will grow to be a big dog.

I put dry puppy food into Molly's bowl. She chews hungrily, making crunchy noises. Soon the bowl is empty. Molly looks at me.

"You want more?" I give her a little more food and a bowl of water. Puppies need lots of fresh water.

Molly rolls the tip of her tongue back, making a cup that catches the water. Ben wants to see Molly drink, but her head disappears in the large bowl.

I rinse her empty food dish. She's my very own puppy to take care of. I'll feed Molly when I'm home, and Mom will look after her when I'm in school.

Molly piddles onto the newspapers. "Mooooom," I call. "Molly went to the bathroom. What do I do?"

"Throw away the wet papers, Jenny. Then wipe the floor with water and a little vinegar and put fresh papers down."

The newspapers are the puppy's bathroom. Slowly we'll put fewer and fewer down until only one corner of the kitchen is covered. Molly will learn to go on the papers and not to go on the floor. It's called *house-training,* or *housebreaking.*

Our kitchen looks funny covered with newspapers. Until the puppy is housebroken we'll play with her here. Ben says, "Let's all be puppies!" We crawl on our hands and knees, making barking sounds. Molly gets excited. She climbs all over us, licking our faces and sniffing our clothes. This is her way of making friends.

When Ben and I get into a fight over Molly, Mom calls from the living room. "Jenny and Ben, leave the puppy alone for a while. Remember, she's not a toy."

At bedtime I say good-night to my puppy.

"Mom, why can't Molly sleep in my room?"

"She has to get used to her own bed, Jenny. Besides, she would piddle onto your rug."

During the night I hear Molly cry. I go to Mom and Dad's bedroom and ask them to come and see if my puppy is sick.

Mom gets up. "Molly's fine," she says. "She's just lonely. In a few days she'll be used to her new home. It's hard to listen to her cry, but if she knows we'll come to comfort her, she won't stop. *Just this once,* we'll go downstairs to Molly."

We talk to her softly. Then we say, "Good-night, Molly," very firmly, and go back upstairs. Mom tucks me under my covers. I snuggle close to my stuffed animals and go back to sleep.

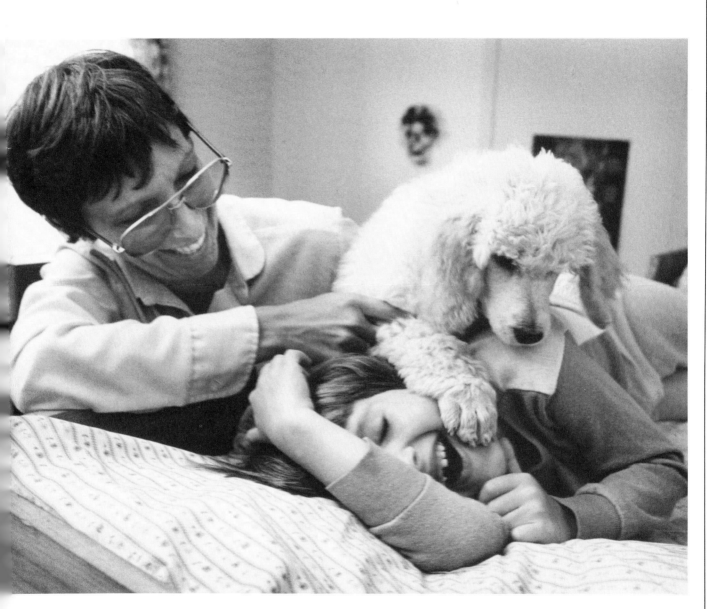

Next morning Mom brings Molly to my bed. "Happy birthday!" Mom sings. I can't believe it! I was so excited about Molly, I forgot that today is my real birthday.

Molly is going outside with us. Dad puts her collar around her neck and clips on the leash. She doesn't like them. First she jumps and then she tries to shake them off. We let her drag the leash around the kitchen. After a while, she calms down, and then we take her outside.

I feel proud when I walk my puppy. I hold the leash just the way Dad shows me. I wish Al were here to see us.

"Hey, Jenny, is that your puppy?" Some of my friends have come to look at Molly.

"Oooh, isn't she cute!" they say, while Molly, as if to show off, makes funny little jumps.

After school on Monday we bring the puppy to Dr. Zausner, a veterinarian whose office is near our school.

"Why does Molly have to see a doctor, Mom? She's not sick."

"A new pet should always be checked by a veterinarian. If Molly ever does get sick, Dr. Zausner can give us advice."

We are called into Dr. Zausner's office. She says hello and asks my puppy's name. Molly sits on the examining table, looking a little scared. Dr. Zausner talks to her softly. With a stethoscope she listens to Molly's heartbeat, feels her belly, and checks her teeth and ears. She makes Molly stand up and then pushes down on her rear end to test the strength of her legs. She feels the bones to see if they are straight and then weighs her.

The doctor asks Mom questions about Molly and writes the information down. Mom gives her a sample of the puppy's bowel movement, which is needed to check for worms.

"What do worms do to a dog?" I ask Dr. Zausner.

"They make a dog sick. Molly should be checked for worms regularly, especially if she is going to play outdoors. If she does get worms, she can be treated with special medicines.

"Now I'm going to give the puppy a shot to protect her from dangerous diseases," Dr. Zausner says.

"Is the shot going to hurt Molly?" I ask.

"No, because I push the needle quickly under the loose skin....See? Molly didn't feel a thing." Dr. Zausner gives Molly a cuddle and tells her she is a good puppy. She asks Mom to bring Molly back for a rabies shot when she is six months old.

I tell Molly that I want to be an animal doctor when I grow up.

Before leaving for school in the morning, I take Molly outside. I don't play with her; I just walk slowly on the grass and let her sniff. Mom says that dogs explore with their sensitive noses as much as with their eyes and ears.

When Molly goes to the bathroom I praise her. Then I pick up after her with a plastic bag, the way my parents showed me. We don't want to leave her mess on the grass or walkway. Taking Molly outside is part of her house-training.

In our fenced-in backyard, Molly can run free. She is full of energy, but, like all puppies, she needs lots of sleep. Mom says Molly naps most of the time I'm at school.

When I come home Molly welcomes me with happy noises. She wags her tail, ready to play. Our favorite game is fetch-the-ball: I roll the ball, Molly picks it up, I take the ball from her mouth. This way she learns I am in charge.

Playing on the floor is easier with newspapers all in one corner. Usually Molly goes to the bathroom on them. When she does, we praise her. But she is not punished if she makes a mistake.

Most puppies love chewing on things. So does Molly,
especially on sneakers. We say NO, take away what she
has in her mouth, and give her a nylon bone instead.

When we play with her, Molly sometimes nips us or
tugs on our clothes. It can hurt. We say NO and stop
playing until she calms down.

Our butcher, Jimmy, puts a bone for Molly in the meat package. It's a shinbone from a cow, the only safe bone for a dog to chew because it doesn't splinter. Mom washes and cooks the bone before giving it to Molly. Chewing on a bone is good for a puppy's teeth.

When I smile, everyone knows I lost another baby tooth. Molly has baby teeth, too. She'll start losing them when she is about five months old, but nobody will notice, because Molly doesn't smile.

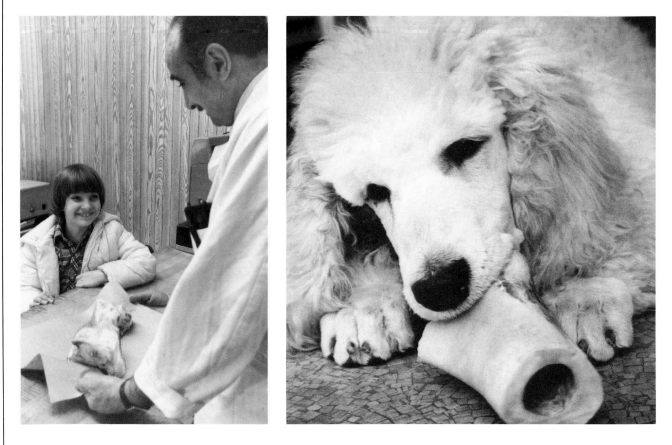

The chilly fall weather doesn't stop Molly and me from playing outside. Running makes both of us feel good. With Molly on a long leash, we chase dry leaves across the park or I throw sticks and Molly fetches them. When we run fast Molly starts panting. She breathes with her mouth open, her pink tongue showing.

I give Molly a big drink of water as soon as we get home.

Molly just tipped over the trash can again. She knows she is not supposed to. Dad puts his hand on her neck and says NO in a slow, deep voice. Molly flattens her ears and tucks in her tail. Poor Molly. I know how it feels to get scolded.

Ben and Molly and I run out to play. When we come in,
Mom says, "Oh, look at you! Two dirty kids and a dirty
puppy. Let's clean you up and then you can help brush
Molly."

Molly stands on a small table in the bathroom. Mom
combs her with a metal comb and brushes her with a
wire brush. This is called *grooming*. It removes dirt and
loose hair. At the same time Mom checks Molly for fleas
and ticks that can easily hide in her thick fur.

Now Mom holds Molly by the collar while Ben and I
take turns brushing and combing. Molly likes it. Her
hair is very soft.

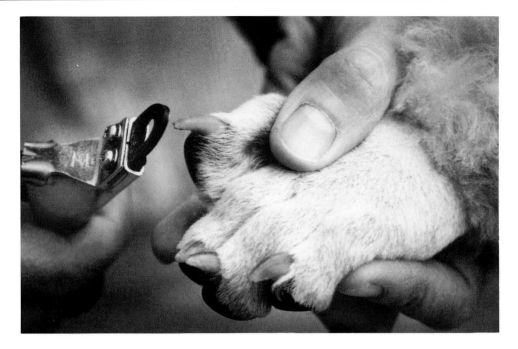

After grooming Mom checks the puppy's ears, teeth, and eyes. If Molly's nails are long, she clips them carefully. Only adults should do this. My parents are right: Caring for a puppy is a lot of work.

Mom says that some people prefer short-haired dogs, because they need less grooming, but not us: We think that long-haired Molly is the prettiest puppy in the world!

When people meet, they say, "Hello, how are you?" When dogs meet, they wag their tails and sniff each other.

On our walks Molly and I meet other people with their dogs. I ask, just to be sure, "Is your dog friendly?" If so, I let Molly get close.

People tell me how nice Molly is and ask me her age and where we got her. Molly is shy. Meeting dogs and people is good for her.

The cold winter weather keeps Molly and me indoors, where it's warm. I'm secretly working on my Christmas presents. Only Molly knows what they are.

Ben and I wrote a letter to Santa, telling him what we would like for Christmas. We added Molly's footprint so Santa will bring her a present, too.

Early Christmas morning Ben and I tiptoe to the living room. Under the tree there are many presents tied with pretty ribbons. "Santa's been here!" we cry.

When Mom and Dad wake up, we get to open our presents. Molly jumps around and plays with the wrapping paper.

"Look, Molly," Dad says. "Santa brought you a bone."

It's nice to share our Christmas with Molly. She doesn't have to stay in the kitchen any longer, because she is house-trained. But if she gets really excited she can have an accident. This is normal, so if it happens we just say NO and quickly take her outside.

One morning, what a surprise! "Ben," I shout, "it's snowing!"

Molly was born in the summer. She has never seen snow. She is surprised and doesn't understand why everything is white. She leaps at snowflakes, sniffs, and kicks up snow with her hind legs. Finally, she rolls in the white powder. What a silly dog!

Ben and I are building a snow castle. Molly tramples right into it.

"No, don't," Ben screams, and pushes her away. "Mooooom, Molly is a pest!"

Mom brings the sled from the house. We pretend Molly is pulling us on a sleigh ride. Mom says that Eskimos, who live in snow houses called igloos, travel on sleds pulled by dog teams. Sled dogs are working dogs. They are not pets like Molly.

Later, Ben and I take warm baths. Molly loves water. She watches us closely and we splash at her. She likes it, but Mom doesn't. Once Molly nearly jumped into the tub with us. That was funny.

Dad says poodles are good swimmers. They were once used for hunting. When hunters shot a wild duck or goose, a poodle would swim out in a lake or pond and return with the dead bird in its mouth. That is called *retrieving*. Poodles are retrievers. That's why Molly returns the sticks I throw.

Dad is home. He says, "Roll up your sleeves, kids. You can help give Molly a bath."

Molly stands in the tub. The lukewarm water is halfway up her legs. Dad makes sure the water is not too hot or too cold. Carefully we wet her coat. Ben and I rub dog shampoo into Molly's dripping fur. In no time Ben's arms, overalls, and cheeks are covered with suds! Dad washes the puppy's face and ears. With a spray attachment, I rinse her coat.

"Do you like it, Molly?" I'm not sure. She is so still, but then she shakes herself and all three of us are wet.

Molly looks so skinny. We rub her dry with clean towels. This she likes. After the bath Molly has to stay indoors for a few hours so she won't catch a cold.

Today is a special day. Mom is taking me to the Westminster Kennel Club Show at Madison Square Garden in Manhattan. She tells me that we are going to see all the different purebred dogs we saw in books before we got Molly.

"Mom, what is a purebred dog?" I ask.

"It is a dog that has been mated with other purebred dogs of the same breed for many generations."

The entrance hall is crowded with people and long lines of dog travel crates with show dogs inside. Their owners are fussing over them. Mom and I walk slowly along the rows, admiring the handsome animals. Mom occasionally exchanges a few words with a breeder.

"These people are experts," she says.

In the back of the hall, professional groomers are making dogs look their most beautiful. It's noisy and busy, but the dogs don't seem to mind.

The dog show takes place in a huge indoor stadium. I hold my mom's hand tightly.

From where we sit I can see that the arena is divided into circles. In each circle a breed of dogs is shown to a judge who is an expert on that breed. He decides which dog comes closest to the *breed standard* and declares that dog the winner. Winners get ribbons. At the end of the competition the most beautiful dog of all the ribbon winners is named the Westminster Champion.

"Mom, I think Molly would be frightened by so many people and dogs."

"I think so, too, but these expensive show dogs are specially trained. Now let's go to the poodle competition."

Mom and I get close to the poodles. The judge is ready. People called *handlers* walk around the ring, leading black or white poodles on thin leashes. A handler's job is to make his or her dog look good in front of the judge. The poodles walk and run, then line up in perfect position, head and tail up. Everybody is quiet while the judge chooses the best dog of the group. The winner is a black poodle. We applaud as he gets his ribbon.

I ask my mom why these poodles have such strange-looking haircuts.

"It's called a *show trim,* Jenny," she answers.

"I like the way Molly looks better," I say.

I'm getting tired. Before we leave, Mom buys a book for Ben, and I buy a treat for Molly.

Molly is still a puppy, but she is strong. When I walk her she pulls, making my arm hurt from holding the leash. I tell her to stop but she keeps doing what she wants. That's no fun.

Mom and Dad decide that Molly and I will go to dog training class. Mom calls a dog obedience school and learns that a beginners' class will start next Saturday.

"Is dog training difficult, Dad?" I ask.

"Everything new takes time to learn, Jenny. We talked to the dog trainer about you and Molly, and she likes to teach children about dog training. She'll be patient. You can do it!"

At the obedience school we meet Liz Gordon, our instructor. Liz explains to us that dogs understand how we feel—they know if we are happy or sad—but they do not understand what we say. When we want them to do something we must teach the right word, called a *command*. A dog learns a command when it is repeated over and over. In a family everybody must use the same commands, or the dog will get confused.

Now Liz shows us how to put a *slip collar* onto our dogs. It's a collar that helps control them.

"Let's teach our dogs the command SIT," Liz says, and explains what to do. I try to follow the instructions, but Molly keeps pulling away. I'm embarrassed, but Liz softly talks to Molly, and she calms down. Liz smiles at me and says, "The first lesson is difficult, but you're doing fine. Dog training is fun. You'll see."

After class, Dad, who has been watching, gives me a hug and says he's proud of me.

Next Saturday Mom comes with me to the training class. Liz says she is glad I'm back, and today the lesson seems easier. I still need help, but Liz never gets impatient with Molly and me.

In every lesson we work on new commands and repeat what we have already learned: COME, SIT, DOWN, HEEL, STAND, STAY. We practice how to hold the leash; how to walk, stand, and turn; and when to use our hands. If my commands are clear Molly will understand them better. Every time Molly does well, I rub her chest and praise her. "Good, Molly," I say. It makes us both feel good.

At home we practice what we learn in class, and I have fun walking Molly again. She is still stronger than I am, but now I can control her. If she pulls I give a quick jerk with the leash. This tightens the slip collar, but it doesn't hurt her. As soon as she slows down, the collar slips loose and she feels comfortable again. Training Molly takes time and patience, but makes her a well-behaved and a happier dog.

Today is our last class. Liz praises Molly and says, "Jenny, I'm very pleased with your work. I hope you will bring Molly for more obedience training when she is an adult dog."

"Can Molly learn tricks?" I ask.

Liz smiles at me. "Definitely. Poodles are playful and smart. They enjoy doing them."

Nothing went right today. At breakfast I spilled my milk. In school the teacher scolded me for talking out of turn. On the way home I had a fight with my friend Catherine, and now Mom sent me to my room because I hit Ben for hiding my snack. Molly knows I'm sad and snuggles close to me. She is warm and soft. I read her a story and begin to feel better. Ben peeks in and says, "I brought you my cookie, Jenny."

Molly barks. I hear a car stop in front of our house. Molly follows me to the door. It's Al! He's here with Trilby!

"Surprise!" Al says with a big smile, and gives me a hug. Then he sees Molly. "Jenny, what a beautiful dog you have. Trilby's been cooped up a long time. Let's take the two of them for a walk."

Molly barks happily. Trilby wags her tail. They sniff each other. Trilby remembers me. She's smaller than I remember her. Al says it's because I'm used to a bigger poodle.

Too soon, Molly and I say good-bye to Al and Trilby.

Molly likes to travel with us. To help her not get carsick, we don't feed her before a trip. We take along plenty of water, though. While the car moves Molly stays in a large wire crate at the back of the station wagon. She can see us and hear us and get plenty of air, but she won't get hurt if the car stops suddenly.

When empty, the crate is easy to fold and carry like a suitcase. At home the crate is Molly's house. It stands in the kitchen and is her favorite spot for taking naps.

"Molly is going to the groomer tomorrow. You want to come?" Mom asks.

"But, Mom, I don't want her to look like the poodles at the show."

"She won't, Jenny, but she needs a trim."

Chip, the dog groomer, knows how to trim all kinds of dogs. His place looks like a beauty salon. Besides combs and brushes, scissors and clippers, he has shampoos, powders, towels, a hair dryer—even a tub.

Chip lifts Molly onto his small grooming table. It has a rubber surface so she won't slip. He puts her onto a leash holder to keep her from turning her head. He works with clippers and scissors to trim her coat, and when he is done Molly looks very pretty. She shakes herself, feeling good.

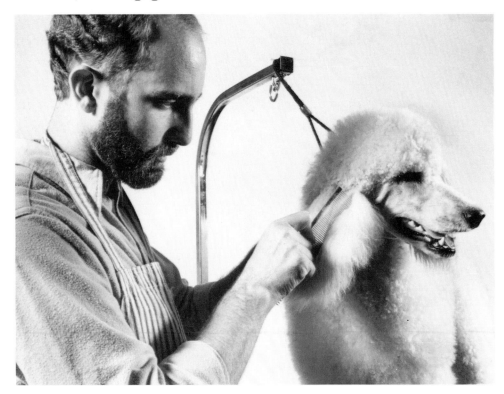

Molly is nine months old and looks like a fully grown dog. But Dad says she is still a "teenager." I remember how small she was on my birthday! Mom tells me that in a few months, when Molly is an adult dog, she will come into *heat*. That means she will be ready to mate and have puppies.

"Can we let Molly have puppies?"

"I don't think so, Jenny. Our house is too small for that."

While Molly is in heat she'll have to be leashed when taken outside because her scent will attract male dogs who will try to mate with her. When it's over after about three weeks, we'll bring her to Dr. Zausner for an operation called *spaying*, after which Molly won't come into heat or have puppies. Molly will stay overnight at the clinic and feel uncomfortable for a day or two, but she will recover quickly.

Finally spring has arrived, and today it's warm and sunny. I put on my favorite yellow shorts and slip into my new sneakers, and off we go, Molly and I, to the nearby park. Molly runs fast, much faster than I do. But she comes back to make sure I keep up with her. When I'm out of breath I rest on the soft grass with Molly next to me. I put my arms around her. We are best friends.

What Parents Should Know

In consultation with Dr. John A. Stetson; Dr. Gail Zausner; Liz Gordon, City Dog Obedience School; and Joe Gordon, Red Doors Kennels

Growing up with a dog is a wonderful learning experience for both child and parents. A puppy becomes a family member for perhaps as long as seventeen years.

Consider before adopting
- ☙ Is your family ready for such a long-term commitment?
- ☙ Is your child who is asking for a puppy at least seven years old and mature enough to handle a dog and help with the chores?
- ☙ Dog care requires a substantial financial commitment: veterinary care, food, grooming, training, boarding, etc. Can you afford it?
- ☙ Does your schedule allow more than just the minimal time to care for your dog? Time for play and affection are very important.
- ☙ Do you have the patience to train your puppy?

How to decide on the right kind of dog
- ☙ Check your public library or bookstore for dog encyclopedias, a good source of accurate information on all breeds. Visit dog shows and obedience trials.
- ☙ Ask yourself: What temperament and characteristics should my dog have? What kind of dog is best suited for my environment, life-style, climate, and my children? Should my family have a male or female dog, a short- or long-haired one, a puppy or an older dog that's already trained?

Where to acquire a dog
- ☙ *Breeders:* If you want a purebred puppy, ask the American Kennel Club, 51 Madison Avenue, New York, NY 10010, for information on reliable breeders in your area. A breeder will help with instructions on raising your puppy and has an interest in the well-being of your dog.
- ☙ *Newspaper ads, neighbors and friends:* Look for a clean place, a healthy litter, and well-behaved, attractive, friendly adult dogs.
- ☙ *Pet stores:* Dog experts generally advise against purchasing a puppy from a pet store.
- ☙ *Veterinarians:* Your local veterinarian knows the breeders in your area. Check his bulletin board for PUPPY FOR SALE notices.
- ☙ *Animal shelters:* Check the shelter; standards vary. Well-run shelters are clean, work with a veterinarian, and have a knowledgeable staff. Make your first visit without your child. Let the staff know what kind of dog you are looking for.

How to choose your dog
- ☙ The signs of good temperament in a dog are friendliness, confidence, playfulness, and curiosity. Stay away from a puppy with runny eyes or nose, discolored teeth, a dull coat or eyes, pale gums, crooked legs, red or bald skin patches, a lump on the tummy; avoid a puppy that is frightened. Observe a litter of puppies closely. Don't pick the most timid or the most aggressive one.
- ☙ *The sale:* Make sure you receive immunization records and a one-day, money-back guarantee that will allow you to have a vet check the puppy. A purebred puppy needs AKC registration papers.
- ☙ *A healthy puppy:* Wherever you buy your puppy, bring it to a veterinarian THE NEXT DAY for a thorough examination. The vet will confirm good health or point out problems. Bring your child along, and ask questions. Return regularly for shots and checkups.

At home
- ☙ Be prepared for the arrival of the puppy. Have a bed ready in a warm, safe, confined living area with an easy-to-clean floor. Puppies have delicate nervous systems; they need lots of sleep. Avoid too much excitement during the first days of adjustment.
- ☙ *Rules for your child*
  A puppy is not a toy: Don't squeeze it; it can get hurt!
  Do not take a dog's food away or play with him while he is eating.
  Do not tease or corner a dog.
  Never strike a dog.
  Do not disturb a sleeping dog.

- *Rules for the puppy:* Do not allow your puppy to establish bad habits like nipping, chewing, and jumping on people or furniture. The parent, not the child, disciplines the dog.
- *Play:* Show your child how to play with the puppy, both indoors and out. Don't permit rough play.
- *Other pets:* Be cautious when introducing your puppy to other pets. Give extra attention to the older animal until the two have accepted each other. Make separate eating arrangements.
- *Diet:* Feed your puppy according to your veterinarian's or breeder's guidelines.
- *Safety indoors:* Keep small chewable items and electrical cords away from a puppy. In your absence leave the puppy in a safe area, preferably in a wire crate. Give him nylon bones for chewing.
- *Safety outdoors:* Leash your dog on the street. Keep your yard free from debris. Lock your gates. Do not allow your dog to roam. Increasingly, dogs of every size and shape are stolen in both urban and rural areas; don't leave your dog unattended. Safely store pesticides, paints, and poisonous chemicals.

How to keep your dog healthy and good-looking
- *Exercise:* Give your puppy frequent, short periods of exercise. Don't overdo it in hot or humid weather; watch for signals from your puppy that he is tired. If your puppy gets wet, dry him with a towel or hair dryer and keep him in a draft-free room.
- *Grooming:* Start grooming early and do it regularly. It benefits a dog's health, cleanliness, and beauty and accustoms him to being handled, which can be helpful in case of injury or sickness. If your dog is long-haired, have him trimmed by a professional groomer, who will instruct you how to keep your dog's coat in good shape. Clip your dog's nails regularly. Be sure to check for parasites and skin irritations. Inspect eyes, ears, teeth and gums, paws, and anus.
- *Parasites:* Fleas and other external parasites are harmful. Ask your veterinarian or breeder for advice.

How to have a well-behaved, happy dog
- *Training:* Formal puppy training may start at three to four months of age. You and your family can learn about dog training from a well-written how-to book. Dog-training schools or clubs may offer what you need. Group classes are most effective. Children are welcome and enjoy them.
- *Car travel:* For your safety and your pet's, a dog belongs in a portable wire travel crate or behind a separation screen in a station wagon. For long-distance trips pack your dog-care equipment: leash, food, water dish, grooming tools, etc. Never leave your dog in a hot, unventilated car.
- *Spaying and neutering:* While your female dog is still a puppy, decide if you will have her spayed and consult your veterinarian, who will decide when to operate. A spayed female dog will not go into heat and have puppies. Male dogs may be neutered when they reach sexual maturity. They will be less inclined to roam and fight with other dogs. Spayed and neutered dogs are happy, devoted pets.

Insurance and licensing
- Your personal liability insurance should cover any damage caused by your dog.
- Dog licensing is obligatory, although regulations vary from community to community. Attach an identification tag to your dog's collar.

Dog shows and obedience trials, a hobby for your child
Children enjoy showing their purebred dogs in Junior Showmanship, or participating—with any kind of dog—in obedience trials. Dog clubs and magazines list these events.

A healthy, well-trained, and affectionate dog is a lovable companion who participates with enthusiasm in a family's activities. The more you and your child know, the more interesting your pet becomes. Take advantage of the many instructive and entertaining books written on puppies and dogs.